SWEDISH ROYAL FAMILY, 1907

MONARCHY

Jennifer Fandel

CREATIVE EDUCATION

Government, in many ways, is like a large family. Just as each family member has a specific role to keep the family unified, governments are comprised of people who

work individually and together to reach common goals. If one or two people don't do their jobs, the whole system can be threatened. Additionally, both families and governments maintain a balance of powers. Just as children look to the leadership of their parents, citizens expect those in the government's top positions to take responsibility for the direction of the country.

The government system called monarchy is built around the idea of family. In this system, however, it's a royal family—a family that typically has historic ties to power and wealth—that represents the interests of the people it governs. The word "monarchy" comes from the Greek word *monarkhia*, meaning "rule of one." In a monarchy, one royal king or queen is the head of the government. While the names "king" and "queen" are common names for a monarch, some countries may use other terms, such as emir, emperor, sultan, raja, czar, or prince. Although in many people's minds the idea of a king or queen seems straight out of a fairy tale, monarchies exist today on almost every continent, in nearly 50 countries, with the largest concentration in the countries of western Europe. Denmark, Britain, the Netherlands, and Spain, among others, have all preserved the rule of monarchy in one way or another.

In some societies, people once believed that monarchs were gods or were appointed by God to take care of the citizens they ruled. Typically, within communities, some families gained wealth and power due to their success in agriculture, and this led to their royal status. Because people had no logical explanation for the families' success, they equated it with a connection to the gods. Eventually, people's beliefs shifted, and what was once considered only a connection to the gods became a god-like position.

RATER · CARNALIS · IO=
I DIVAE · VIRG · MARIÆ

I
IACOBVS · MINOR · EPVS · MARIA · CLEOPHÆ
HIEPOSOLIMITANVS · VIRG · MAR · PVTATT
TERTERA · D

III
IOSEPH · IVSTVS · SIMON · ZELOTES · CONSO=

FAMILY OF HOLY ROMAN EMPEROR MAXIMILIAN I (LEFT)

This belief in a god-like monarch was very common in ancient Egypt, Greece, and Rome, as well as within some parts of the Middle East and Asia. People prayed to and made sacrifices for their king, hoping that he would bestow goodness upon them. They relied on him for good weather and a plentiful harvest. If things stopped going well, people often looked with suspicion at the monarch, believing that that person was no longer chosen by God to lead the nation. In situations such as these, the monarch was often overthrown or sacrificed by the people. While belief in a monarch's connection to the gods is rare today, it still exists in Tibet, where followers of the Dalai Lama, the country's spiritual and political leader, believe that his body contains the Buddhist spirit of compassion.

Commonly, monarchs come from families with money and power. The history of a monarch is usually long and well-documented, showing connections to royal bloodlines or dynasties of the past. In most cases, the crown is passed down within a family in a process known as hereditary succession. A monarch typically stays in power until she or he dies, abdicates, or, in some cases, is overthrown.

Throughout history, countries have often changed laws regarding hereditary succession. At one time, it was common for countries to follow the law of primogeniture, which states that the crown must be passed down to the firstborn male child in the royal family. If there were no male children in the family, male cousins had the chance to inherit the crown. However, even if countries followed the law of primogeniture, they occasionally overlooked it to allow women who were well-liked to become the ruling monarch. Such was the case for Queen Isabella (1451–1504) of Castile, a province of Spain, who inherited the crown when her half-brother died. When she married King Ferdinand (1452–1516) of Aragón, both the king and queen kept their positions, ruling the two Spanish provinces together. In modern times, the order of birth, regardless of gender, typically determines who becomes a country's king or queen. For example, Denmark's present queen,

Spain

King James VI (1566–1625) of Scotland, who later became King James I of England, reigned from 1567 to 1625. In this excerpt from *A Speech to the Lords and Commons of Parliament at White-Hall*, the king explains his views of divine right.

"The state of monarchy is the supremest thing upon Earth. For kings are not only God's lieutenants upon Earth, and sit upon God's throne, but even by God himself are called gods. . . .

King James I

"Kings are justly called gods for that they exercise a manner or resemblance of divine power upon Earth. For if you will consider the attributes to God, you shall see how they agree in the person of a king. God has power to create, or destroy, make, or unmake at his pleasure, to give life, or send death, to judge all, and to be judged nor **accountable** to none; to raise low things, and to make high things low at his pleasure, and to God are both souls and body due. And the like power have kings: they make and unmake their subjects, they have power of raising and casting down, of life and of death; judges over all their subjects, and in all cases, and yet accountable to none but God only."

QUEEN MARGRETHE II OF DENMARK

Margrethe II (1940–), inherited the crown as the firstborn child in her family.

Most monarchies throughout history have fallen into one of two broad categories: absolute monarchy or constitutional monarchy. In an absolute monarchy, the king or queen makes the laws, enforces the laws, and interprets the laws. The monarch answers to no one. Absolute monarchies were especially common in the 16th and 17th centuries, and monarchs often followed a doctrine called divine right. This meant that the monarchs—and often their followers—believed that the decisions they made came straight from God. What the king or queen said was law, whether or not it was in the best interest of the country.

In most absolute monarchies, a close staff of **nobility** carries out the orders of the monarch. These nobles may serve in high government positions, taking care of their country's finances, foreign relations, defense, or law and justice. For example, in the Middle Eastern country of Qatar, relatives of the king and the country's elite help rule the country. While most nobles don't speak out against the monarch for fear of losing their positions, those who question or disobey him are often strictly punished. In Medieval Europe, it was not always easy to gain a noble position in the court of a monarch. Not only did one need to have money and influence, but a person had to agree with the ideals of the monarch. Spain's King Philip II (1527–98) made following his religion, Catholicism, a requirement for earning his favor.

In most absolute monarchies, there is a large divide in income and status between the citizens and the monarch. Usually, the wealth is in the hands of the monarch and a small upper class, while the rest of the citizens live completely dependent on the land. This is part of how absolute monarchs retain their power: the citizens, many of them poor, don't believe they have the power to challenge the rich, powerful monarchy.

At times, however, absolute monarchs have been challenged—and even overthrown. During the Enlightenment of the 1700s, for example, citizens throughout

Denmark

Europe demanded more personal rights and more involvement in their government. Monarchs who failed to listen often found themselves removed from the throne, as did King Louis XVI (1754–93) during the French Revolution of 1789, in which the monarchy was overthrown and a republic established.

Other absolute monarchs of the Enlightenment period gave up some of their power, granting people limited rights. These monarchs are often called enlightened despots, or enlightened absolutists. One enlightened despot was King Frederick II (1712–86), who reformed laws and modified the punishments for violations of those laws during his 18th-century reign in Prussia, once an independent German state. Frederick's reforms, in addition to his efforts to strengthen Prussia's educational system and create new industries, helped draw his citizens' attention to the positive aspects of the monarchy.

Many absolute monarchs throughout history have allowed their countries to become constitutional monarchies, accepting an elected government while holding on to their money, property, and place in society. Today, the majority of monarchies still in existence are constitutional monarchies. In this type of monarchy, the monarch has a limited role in the governing of a country, mostly serving as a figurehead or advisor. Overall, there is a separation of powers. While the monarch is considered the head of state with powers over the **executive branch**, his or her power is typically ceremonial. For instance, the monarch may sign laws or officially begin a new session of parliament, but he or she has no independent power and is not allowed to take actions such as vetoing laws. Rarely, the monarch may play an important role in breaking a deadlock in parliament.

Rather than wielding true power, the constitutional monarch's governmental work is in the form of a royal stamp of approval. The real control of the country rests in the hands of the prime minister and elected officials in parliament, who are responsible for taxation and lawmaking, and the people who elect them. The

France

PEASANTS IN THE FRENCH REVOLUTION, 1789

monarch's only real power is over the decisions made within the royal family, and even these decisions are subject to criticism from lawmakers and private citizens. Because citizens typically pay taxes to maintain the property and livelihood of the royal family, many believe that the royal family is responsible to them. To these people, the royal family is their family, too.

THE RULE OF THE CROWN

Under the earliest monarchies, dating back more than 5,000 years—and even under those that flourished only a few centuries ago—life was often difficult for the majority of the population. Because monarchs rose to their position by virtue of their power and wealth, they usually lived carefree lives quite removed from their citizens. Thus, monarchs had little concept of what life was like for the people they governed, who were often poor. The kings of many nations placed high taxes on their subjects, most of whom worked as farmers or laborers. Rather than providing necessities such as food and adequate shelter for the country's citizens, these high taxes kept the monarch finely robed, well fed, and pampered.

In the few absolute monarchies that still exist today, people often find themselves living in hardship as well. In addition to suffering from class divisions, which keep money and power in the hands of a very small group, citizens of an absolute monarchy often have few rights, although this varies depending on the personality and philosophy of the monarch. Because an absolute monarch typically rules over his country with an iron fist, centralizing his power and maintaining it through a well-developed military, citizens are at his mercy. People have no way to state their opinions about—let alone change—the government, as political parties and elections don't exist in an absolute monarchy.

Absolute monarchs are usually in control of their country's finances, and this

France

KING LOUIS XVI OF FRANCE

Only five absolute monarchies exist today, and most of them are centered in the Middle East and Asia. In the Middle East, Saudi Arabia and Qatar most closely fit the profile of an absolute monarchy. In Asia, Brunei stands out for the amount of power resting in the sultan's hands. All of these countries share one thing in common: they sit on large reserves of oil. As has been true throughout history, absolute monarchies typically thrive when there is a large divide between the rich and the poor. In each of these countries, the royal family has ownership and control of the oil reserves and the oil industry.

Saudi Arabia

Brunei, however, does something different than its absolute counterparts in the Middle East. While Sultan Hassanal Bolkiah (1946–) is one of the richest people in the world, he shares his wealth among his citizens. The sultan has improved his people's lives by providing free medical care (even special treatment abroad) and free education through the university level. Does he do this to better his country? Or does he hope that providing these services will keep people happy with his absolute reign? No one but the sultan truly knows.

SULTAN HASSANAL BOLKIAH OF BRUNEI

position of power is often abused. In many circumstances, absolute monarchs use the country's money to fund their own private—and often foolhardy—interests, spending money on themselves first and then using whatever is left over for their country. For example, in building the palace Versailles, King Louis XIV (1638–1715) dragged France into a $21-million debt. Today, Swaziland's King Mswati III (1968–) lives lavishly and has bought—among other extravagant things—a $500,000 car, while 70 percent of his citizens live on less than $1 a day. In some cases, such a show of wealth is intended to prove the monarch's power, heightening the perception of distance between the rich, powerful king and his poor and lowly subjects. In other cases, monarchs spend money on themselves out of simple greed. Absolute monarchs also often play favorites with their money and power, giving common citizens the impression that their needs will be ignored and their problems misunderstood. These impressions are often true.

THE PALACE OF VERSAILLES IN FRANCE

While the citizens of absolute monarchies often find that their basic needs are not met, those living in constitutional monarchies usually enjoy a high standard of living. The lawmaking branch of the government, most often the parliament, typically upholds laws to preserve **democratic** rights for the country's people, including free speech, freedom of religion, an open media, the right to protest and assemble, and the right to vote. In fact, most constitutional monarchies are known to have excellent **human rights** records.

While constitutional monarchies do have better human rights standards than many other types of governments in the world, some still deal with discrimination problems. Because of the stability of many of the world's constitutional monarchies, these governments often welcome immigrants from other countries. At times, however, discrimination on the part of the country's citizens makes it difficult for those of different **ethnic** backgrounds to find work, housing, and even acceptance in their new countries. Most constitutional monarchies try to restrict or even abolish discrimination, and those in power—both in the parliament and in the monarchy—have often stepped up to serve as a positive example for their citizens. This was true during World War II, for example, when Queen Wilhelmina (1880–1962) of the Netherlands encouraged the protection of the Jews in her country.

Under constitutional monarchies, citizens are allowed to vote for their elected officials, although they are not allowed to vote for or against the monarchy. The monarchy remains in place, unless there is significant action by both lawmakers and citizens to abolish it. In modern times, this is quite rare. Most monarchs would rather make adjustments to remedy citizen discontent than lose their position in the country. For instance, during the 1980s, when Britain struggled with massive unemployment, many citizens campaigned to get rid of the monarchy. Because many of the citizens' complaints related to the royal family's wealth, Queen Elizabeth II (1926–) volunteered to pay taxes, just like everyone else.

Netherlands

A CEREMONY HONORING THE KING OF SWAZILAND

TRIBAL KINGS

African monarchs have played an important part in government throughout the continent's history. Until the late 19th century, when Europeans set up colonies in Africa, much of the continent was governed by tribal kings. These kings each ruled over a specific territory, creating and enforcing laws for their people, who usually shared a common language or culture.

Swaziland

When Europeans came to Africa, most recognized the importance of the tribal kingdoms. They incorporated the kings into their government, making them administrators of specific territories. Even once African nations gained independence from the Europeans in the 20th century, the tribal kings were still recognized by the people. They were considered ceremonial rulers of specific ethnic groups.

The country of Swaziland has managed to take the concept of tribes and chiefs, or kings, much further than many of its African neighbors. The country is divided into 40 chieftaincies (tribal provinces), and each chieftaincy sends two members to elect the head chief, or king, of the country. However, since the king has the power to choose the tribal representatives in each of the provinces, the effectiveness of this system is presently being debated within the country. As Swaziland transitions to a more democratic system, the government will likely try to limit the king's influence.

Even though citizens cannot vote monarchs out of their positions, they are fully allowed to express their views about the royal family, the government, and any other issue on their minds. There are no limits placed on free speech. Additionally, there is full freedom of the press. While responsible journalism is strongly favored, this responsibility is enforced from within the media. The media is held to its own high standards of accurate reporting, and the government must answer to reports uncovered by journalists. In most countries with a constitutional monarchy, the government has an open relationship with the press and provides information freely in order to have it shared with the country's citizens.

Under constitutional monarchies, freedom of religion is also important, although some countries claim one church as the country's established church. Under this system, citizens are allowed to believe and worship as they like, but the monarch must be an official member of the designated church. For example, the Lutheran Church of Norway is that country's official church, and the **constitution** requires that the monarch be a member of the church. Those within the royal family, including those who marry into the family, are expected to claim Lutheranism, a type of Christian religion, as their own.

Property ownership is also common under constitutional monarchies. Citizens are allowed to own their own property and maintain it as they see fit. Property is transferred between private individuals, rather than from the government, although taxes for necessities such as education, healthcare, and roadways are typically paid to the government. The property of the monarch is the only exception to private ownership. Much of the monarch's property, including land and estates, is said to belong to the country. If the monarch were to leave his position, he couldn't sell these pieces of property, which must remain within the royal family. At the same time, however, citizens are not allowed to demand access to the property, even though they pay to maintain it. The same is true for lawmakers. While they have a

Norway

PRINCESS MARTHA LOUISE OF NORWAY

higher position than ordinary citizens, even they do not have access to the monarch's property.

In most countries with constitutional monarchies, the royal family sits at or near the very highest income bracket in the country. The rest of the wealth in constitutional monarchies is fairly evenly distributed, however, although this is often due to the economic systems, such as capitalism, that these countries have in place. Many constitutional monarchies, such as Norway and Canada, operate as welfare states, meaning that the government gives all citizens equal access to healthcare, education, employment, and cultural programs. Although this system doesn't evenly distribute the wealth in a country, it ensures that all people—regardless of social status or income—get the basic services they need.

In some constitutional monarchies, citizens still perceive large class differences, as wealthy families often have greater access to expensive private schools and can make connections with others at the "top" of society. These connections keep the benefits of wealth and power at the higher levels of society, providing better jobs and more opportunities within this close-knit circle. Those at the bottom of the spectrum may not have more than a basic education, and this, along with their lack of money and connections, means they have little opportunity to advance. The story of the poor entrepreneur whose hard work led to wealth is nearly unheard of in England, as both the government and society as a whole bestow favor upon those with high education levels and wealth.

Despite class and economic differences between citizens and the royalty, the balance of power is one of the leveling factors in constitutional monarchies. Because citizens hold the power to vote for or against officials in the government, they have the final say in how their government works. In many ways, the monarchy stands officially at the side of the government, giving its long-range perspective, but expressing few of its own biases.

Canada

Countries with monarchies have long debated the necessity of maintaining this type of government. Throughout history, some citizens have fought to get rid of the monarchy, while others have fought to preserve it. In the 1700s, this debate electrified citizens in the American colonies, which were then under the power of the British monarchy. In 1776, when the colonies ratified the Declaration of Independence, their relationship with the British crown was severed.

For the American **colonists** who wanted to establish a nation independent from the British monarchy, three key issues formed the premise of their argument: they believed in the idea of a representative government, they opposed the high British taxes imposed on them, and they wanted a **legislative** system that treated people as equals, regardless of their wealth or status in society. Many of the modern debates about the necessity of a monarchy revolve around these same three issues.

Those who oppose monarchies often do so because they don't believe that this government system fairly represents their interests. They think that a system that supports a monarchy—both financially and legally—cannot also do a good job of addressing the needs of its people. These detractors also contend that there's little need to keep such an outdated and impractical system alive, as having a monarch open a session of parliament or put his or her official seal of approval on a bill does nothing to keep the lawmaking branches of government working effectively.

Additionally, many people question whether a royal family can truly represent the concerns of the average citizen. Because of their wealth—Liechtenstein's royal family, for example, is worth an estimated $4.6 billion—members of the royal family don't have to deal with the difficulties of daily life, such as unemployment, taking care of a family, or paying for basic necessities. Many view the royal family as out of touch with ordinary life. Eighteenth-century French philosopher Jean Jacques Rousseau (1712–78) addressed this disconnect between monarchs and their

Liechtenstein

Throughout history, strict rules have defined royal relationships. At one time, royal families tried to keep their bloodlines as pure as possible by setting up marriages between their children and their royal cousins in other countries. Additionally, this ensured that the royal family would keep its power and wealth.

In the 1520s, King Henry VIII (1491–1547) of England started a controversy in the English monarchy when he divorced his first wife, Catherine of Aragón (1485–1536). Because Catherine could not produce an heir to the throne, Henry wanted the marriage declared invalid. The pope, however, would not grant the divorce, and Henry split from the Catholic Church. Under his reign, the Church of England was formed. Henry married five more times.

United Kingdom

After Henry VIII's actions, divorce was not taken lightly in England. In 1937, the English Parliament forced King Edward VIII (1894–1972) to abdicate when he announced his upcoming marriage to a divorced American woman. This was the first abdication ever of the British throne. More recently, when Britain's Prince Charles (1948–) and Princess Diana (1961–97) announced their divorce in 1996, the country's citizens and the queen made their discontent known.

WEDDING OF PRINCE CHARLES AND PRINCESS DIANA

subjects in his book *Confessions*, in which he told the story of a princess who, upon hearing that the peasants were poor and had no bread, said, "Let them eat cake." The princess, so removed from the peasants' lives, didn't understand that having no bread, a staple item in peasants' diets, meant having very little to eat. Eating cake, obviously, wasn't a choice for people who couldn't afford the most basic necessities. This saying has been falsely attributed to Marie Antoinette (1755–93), the 18th-century queen of France, likely because she didn't understand the lives of the poor people she governed.

In addition to the representation problem is the cost of maintaining the monarchy. The funds used to keep the royal family living in splendor come from taxpayers, and lawmakers have the difficult work of justifying tax increases to cover these costs. In the Netherlands, for example, about $7.1 million was paid to the queen, prince, and princess in 2006 for their annual living allowance. Some countries also permit their monarchs to make additional tax-free income on their property, estates, and investments.

Many who wish to abolish constitutional monarchies also believe that it's contradictory to have a monarchy—a system that historically tried to separate itself from the people—working hand-in-hand with a democratic government, which encourages the participation of all of its citizens. Such was the argument of Thomas Paine (1737–1809), a writer who emigrated from England to the United States in 1774. In his popular political pamphlet *Common Sense*, he argued for the abolishment of the monarchy: "To the evil of monarchy we have added that of hereditary succession; and as the first is a degradation and lessening of ourselves, so the second, claimed as a matter of right, is an insult and imposition on posterity [generations to come]. For all men being originally equals, no one by birth could have a right to set up his own family in perpetual preference to all others." To Paine and many others, a monarchy—no matter what form it may take—would always emphasize the deep

France

social inequalities that democracy tried to level out.

Despite the disadvantages of monarchies, many citizens who live under monarchies view the system as purely positive. Some see the monarchy as a continual symbol of their country and its history. For these people, there is value in keeping the links between the past and present alive. They often see the monarchy as a part of their own identity as citizens, revealing that they cherish their past and wish to share it with others. Those in favor of the monarchy also contend that their monarch is a unifying presence in the country, as most monarchs believe that it is their duty to remain free of political views. This broadens their appeal among citizens, who

QUEEN MARIE ANTOINETTE OF FRANCE

might be divided by their support for or disagreement with elected officials. Some people also find comfort in knowing that while prime ministers and members of parliament come and go, the royal family will endure.

Additionally, in many countries ruled by monarchies today, tourism is a major aspect of the economy. As representatives of a people and their culture, the monarchy often attracts attention—and tourists—to these countries. For example, England's Buckingham Palace, the London residence of the royal family, welcomes around 500,000 invited guests each year, and likely another 500,000 visit as tourists. Without a monarch breathing life into old palaces, many people fear that tourists would gradually lose interest and take their tourism money elsewhere.

Perhaps the most important benefits to those who live under constitutional monarchies are the specific charitable, educational, and cultural programs that are managed or funded by the royal family. Monarchs try to make connections with the

BUCKINGHAM PALACE IN LONDON

people in their countries by making donations, being present at and sponsoring charity events, visiting the poor and sick, and appearing at high-profile sporting or arts events. The late Princess Diana felt strongly about the British royal family's role as humanitarians and encouraged greater activism. She once said, "Being constantly in the public eye gives me a special responsibility . . . to transmit a message, to sensitize the world to an important cause, to defend certain values."

A monarch's dedication to charitable programs can also benefit the parliamentary leaders in constitutional monarchies. By allowing the monarch to serve as the public face of the government's charitable work, as many constitutional monarchies do, some of the pressures typically placed on members of parliament and the prime minister are alleviated. Lawmakers who might normally take time out of their schedules to spread positive publicity about their country or appear at official ceremonies or fundraisers can leave much of this work to the monarch. Additionally, monarchs can serve as diplomats, helping to establish peaceful relations and exchange ideas with countries around the globe.

Yet, despite these benefits, the monarchy can also cause lawmakers difficulties. Citizens may split their attention and loyalties between the government and the crown, making it difficult for lawmakers to hold the public's attention on important issues. Many people spend their time following the royal family and its real-life soap opera—just as they did in 2001 when Norway's Prince Haakon (1973–) announced his scandal-ridden engagement to an unwed mother—rather than the proceedings of parliament. Likewise, the government may find itself answering for or explaining the royalty's decisions. This was the case in 2003, when the Dutch prime minister had to account for government spying on Queen Beatrix's niece and her fiancé. While the queen had ordered the spying to make sure that her niece's future husband was appropriate for the royal family, many citizens felt that it was an inappropriate use of the government's intelligence services.

United Kingdom

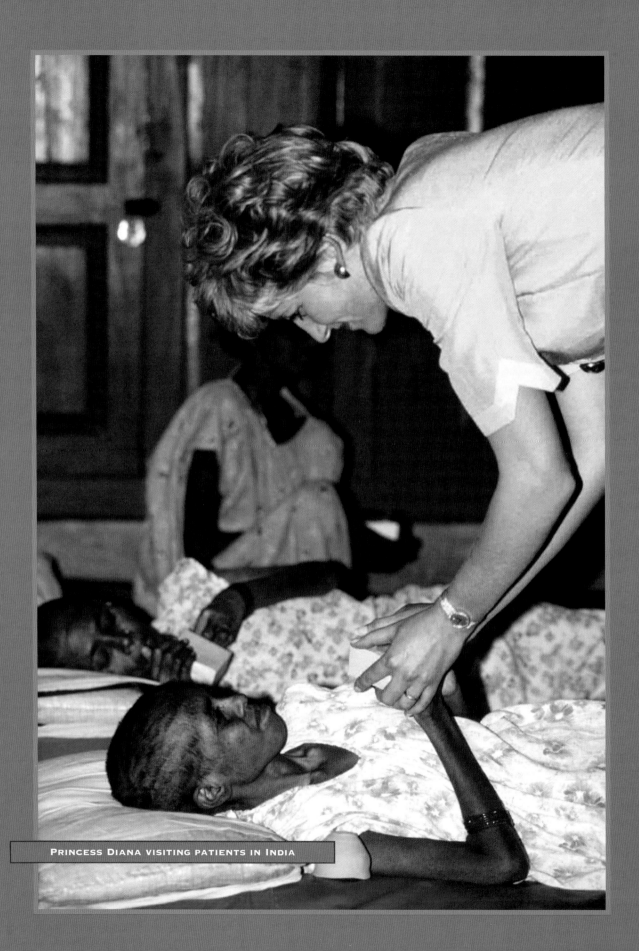

PRINCESS DIANA VISITING PATIENTS IN INDIA

In modern times, most royal families feel that they need to maintain public support for their position in the country by serving the public. Most monarchs are involved with volunteer organizations both within and outside of their countries. A monarch well known for her dedication to humanitarian efforts was the late Princess Diana of Wales. In her lifetime, Princess Diana volunteered for more than 100 charities. Banning the use and manufacture of land mines was particularly important to her, and she spent time visiting land mine survivors and campaigning against land mine use. She also publicized the need for more funding and care for the homeless, dying, and sick, especially those with HIV/AIDS.

Sweden

Royalty in other countries have also felt compelled to serve others. In Norway, Princess Martha Louise (1971–) served as a goodwill ambassador for the United Nations in 1992 and visited refugee camps in villages between the Ivory Coast and Liberia in Africa. In Sweden, King Carl XVI Gustaf (1946–) is actively involved in environmental causes, and his wife, Queen Silvia (1943–), founded the World Childhood Foundation in 1999 to help provide better living conditions for children around the world. She is also active in campaigns to help disabled children in her country.

Whether they're supported or denounced by the people and lawmakers who live within them, constitutional monarchies today enjoy widespread support by most countries around the globe. The monarchy, by keeping alive many of a country's rich traditions, is a piece of living history from which people around the world can learn. In many cases, decisions made centuries ago still affect the way people, cultures, and conflicts are viewed today. Also, most constitutional monarchies are stable governments that have worked hard to preserve the balance of power between the parliament, the citizens, and the royal family. This stability translates into reasonable and accountable governments on the world stage, and countries with stable governments often engage in fewer conflicts both within the country and abroad.

FROM CROWN TO SHINING CROWN

Monarchies are one of the oldest types of government. During the years 3200 to 2350 B.C., some of the world's first known governments emerged in Mesopotamia (modern-day Iraq). Before this time, people organized themselves loosely in small, local tribes in which the tribal chief held the position of power, and this power was often passed down within his family.

The first governments were shaped as a Mesopotamian people called the Sumerians built the first cities, which had walls to keep out invaders. Different from agricultural communities of the past in which most families were self-sufficient, the Sumerian cities were characterized by their division of labor, with people specializing in a variety of jobs. The division of labor led to an overall increase in wealth, which attracted both thieves and power-hungry conquerors from outside the city. The Sumerians realized that they needed protection, in the form of a military, for their property and wealth. Additionally, because conflicts arose between citizens of the city, a system to calm these conflicts and develop ways of resolving them was needed. Thus, the first governments were formed.

The earliest governments in the Sumerian cities were most likely made up of assemblies of wealthy and powerful men. In many cases, these men had been tribal leaders in the past. They made decisions for the cities, although they appointed a handful of people within the assembly to take care of the government in times of crisis. Eventually, these appointed individuals took over, establishing themselves as kings. Around 3000 B.C., all Sumerian cities had kings that claimed absolute authority over their area.

After 2350 B.C., the cities of Mesopotamia were transformed into regional **empires**. Sargon of Akkad (c. 2300s–2200s B.C.) created one such empire, which grew under his control. He took over cities and strengthened his rule by creating a large, powerful army. Additionally, he tried to centralize the government under his power by controlling and taxing trade, which made the capital city of Akkad the wealthiest and most powerful city in the world at that time. Lasting several generations, Sargon's empire gradually weakened because of outside invasions. By 2000 B.C., the empire had collapsed.

Since the earliest monarchies, centralizing the government has been one of the best ways for monarchs to increase their power and build strong and lasting governments. One country that mastered the centralized government was France under the leadership of King Louis XIII (1601–43), who reigned from 1610 to 1643, and his son Louis XIV, known as the "Sun King." The mastermind of King Louis XIII's reign was his chief minister, the Catholic Church official Cardinal Richelieu (1585–1642). Richelieu did everything he could to keep track of the government and handpicked commoners loyal to the king to work as government **bureaucrats**. Additionally, he selected officials to supervise the bureaucracy and make sure that royal policies were being enforced.

Before Louis XIII's reign, the nobility still held positions of power within the country. Richelieu, however, saw these people as a threat to the government and did everything he could to rid France of their power and influence. He ordered their castles destroyed, crushed conspiracies to gain power, and even attacked the nobles' allies to drain their political and military power. While much of Richelieu's plan revolved around destroying the power of nobles, he also encouraged the nobles to accept the king's rule through bribes.

Later, when Louis XIV came to power in 1643, he declared that he and he alone was the government of France. His ultimate exhibition of wealth and power was seen in his palace at Versailles, outside of Paris. Commissioned in the 1670s, the palace became the largest building in Europe. Prominent nobles and their families were encouraged to live at Versailles, which allowed the king to keep an eye on them. In exchange for the rich living quarters, Louis was essentially given permission to run the country without the nobles' interference.

During King Louis XIV's reign, monarchs in Austria, Prussia, and Russia looked to France as a model of centralized government. Louis and his advisors put through many new laws, controlled the large standing army to keep order in France, established new industries, and built roads and canals. The king also started wars to enlarge French boundaries. His hope was to establish France as the dominant power in Europe.

More than 100 years later, ideas of the Enlightenment began to affect governments in Europe and Russia. In countries where the Enlightenment ideals of rational thought and personal rights caught on, a number of absolute monarchs modified their leadership role. In particular, in Russia, Catherine the Great (1729–96) exemplified the role of the "enlightened despot."

Catherine the Great (also known as Catherine II) ruled Russia from 1762 to 1796. Like Peter the Great (1672–1725) before her, she wanted to make the government

France

KING LOUIS XIV OF FRANCE

EMPEROR PU YI OF CHINA

EMPIRES & DYNASTIES

Japan and China were once famous for their long-ruling empires and lasting dynasties. For 4,000 years, beginning around 2000 B.C., a succession of dynasties ruled China, with each requiring strict obedience to the government. The downfall of the dynasties occurred because of government corruption and a weak military, which was unable to keep out foreigners. In 1911, citizens demanded a better government and forced the last emperor, Pu Yi (1906–67), to abdicate when he was only six years old. In time, China became a **communist** country.

Japan

In Japan, a line of rulers called the House of Yamato established its kingdom in the fifth century A.D., and that kingdom kept its position in the country until 1946. Believing that they were descended from the sun god Yamato, Japan's emperors had absolute political and religious power in the country. In 1946, after Japan's defeat in World War II, Emperor Hirohito (1901–89) was forced to give up his position as "god king." This meant that he had to give up most of his powers and his claim to divine right in the country. Japan is now governed as a constitutional monarchy.

EMPRESS CATHERINE THE GREAT OF RUSSIA

more efficient. To do this, she divided Russia into 50 administrative territories and appointed bureaucrats to be in charge of each one. Additionally, she defined the rights and responsibilities of the nobility. While she gave the noble landowners more power over their own lands and rights over the peasants who worked those lands, she also expected the nobility to follow her orders.

What made Catherine the Great's reign special in comparison to other absolute monarchs was the influence of the Enlightenment on her government. She wanted policies that would improve her citizens' lives, and she brought better education systems and support of the arts and literature to her citizens. Additionally, she restricted the punishments that could be used on the peasants, doing away with beatings, torture, and, in many cases, the death penalty. Nonetheless, she knew where to draw the line with her ideas. While she wanted to improve the lives of those she governed, her motives weren't entirely pure. She believed that keeping her citizens happy would allow her to retain her power at a time when people throughout Europe were questioning the role of the monarch in government. For the most part, she was right. Her reign was generally harmonious until the end of the 1700s, when rebellions, likely influenced by independence movements in Europe, broke out in Russia. Afraid of losing her power completely, Catherine tightened her rule.

The monarchy eventually died out in Mesopotamia, France, and Russia, but it has maintained its stronghold in Britain even today. Britain's monarchy is a good example of how adaptation to change is necessary in order for governments to survive intact. While England was governed by an absolute monarchy for around 800 years, it allowed a parliament to develop in the 13th century, although it was under the governance of the king. After a dispute between the king and Parliament broke into civil war (1642–49), England's constitutional monarchy was formed. In 1688, Parliament overthrew King James II (1633–1701) and took over as the head of government. In 1689, two important documents in the British constitution, the

Russia

Declaration of Rights and the Bill of Rights, went into effect in England. While the documents allowed placing a monarch back on the throne, they gave ultimate law-making and law-enforcing power to Parliament. After this time, Parliament's power was never again challenged in England.

Today, the reach of Britain's monarchy extends to nearly every continent on the globe. Britain, which once sat at the helm of a large colonial empire, still has connections to many of the countries that were once under its power. At present, 17 of the 50 countries in the world ruled by monarchies are under the reign of the British monarchy. Queen Elizabeth II serves as the head of state for the United Kingdom, which includes England, Scotland, Wales, and Northern Ireland. Additionally, she is the head of state for 16 other countries, including Canada and Australia. The majority of these countries have their own independent parliaments and regard the British monarch—just as the British do—as a figurehead.

At one time, monarchies dominated the globe, but their influence has faded with their decreasing numbers. Yet, they hold an interesting position in the world. With one foot in the past and another in the present, monarchies stand as a testament to their history and their ongoing relationship with the people they represent. Likely, if they maintain their friendship with their citizens and continue to be shining examples of their countries' history and culture, their place in society will remain untouched.

United Kingdom

QUEEN ELIZABETH II OF BRITAIN, 1953

3000 B.C.

Monarchies begin in Mesopotamia (modern-day Iraq).

2000 B.C.

The Mesopotamian empire of Sargon of Akkad collapses.

660 B.C.

Emperors begin ruling Japan.

206 B.C.

The Han dynasty in China gets its start.

A.D. **700–800**

A monarch-based government begins in Britain.

1066

William, Duke of Normandy, conquers England, becoming king.

1502

The last Aztec emperor of Mexico, Montezuma, comes to power; his reign will last 18 years.

1643

King Louis XIV begins his 72-year reign as France's "Sun King."

1688

In England, the Declaration of Rights and the Bill of Rights go into effect;
power begins to shift to Parliament.

1762

Catherine the Great begins her 34-year reign as an "enlightened despot" in Russia.

1776

The British monarchy loses control of the American colonies when the
Declaration of Independence is signed and made official.

The French Revolution begins, eventually leading to the end of France's absolute monarchy.

1803

French military general Napoleon Bonaparte crowns himself emperor; his reign will last until 1815.

The last Chinese dynasty comes to an end.

1917

The absolute monarchy in Russia is overthrown;

parties struggle to establish communist and republic governments.

Japan

1946

Japan's Emperor Hirohito gives up his rule as "god king" of the country.

India is granted independence from the British monarchy and becomes a democratic republic.

Elizabeth II becomes queen of Great Britain and Northern Ireland.

Spain

King Juan Carlos has his position restored as Spain's monarch

nearly 45 years after the monarchy was deposed in 1931.

1997

Britain's beloved Princess Diana dies in a car crash.

King Abdullah of Saudi Arabia

abdicates Steps down or resigns from a position as the head of a monarchy. Monarchs may be pressured to abdicate by the government, the royal family, or even the public.

accountable Held to account. Someone who is accountable is available to answer questions about his or her actions and is prepared to take responsibility for their consequences.

bloodlines A family's line of descendents. Most royal families keep family trees that trace their bloodlines back many centuries.

bureaucrats Administrators in a bureaucracy, a huge, complex system of government with many rules and many people with specialized functions.

capitalism An economic system built on individual investment in enterprise and private ownership. Those who use the system are called capitalists.

centralizing Locating the government in a specific place. Centralized governments, often based in a capital city, make decisions for the whole country, instead of letting regional governments make their own laws.

colonists People who travel to a distant place and establish a new community but are still governed by their home country.

communist A term used to describe a system of government that discourages private ownership of property and enterprise. Instead, the government manages property and enterprise on behalf of its citizens.

constitution The basic ideas by which a country is governed, particularly as they relate to the powers of government and the rights of citizens.

democratic A term used to describe governments based on citizen participation. In most democracies, citizens vote for officials to represent their interests.

dynasties Successions of rulers from one family, which usually has great wealth or prominence in society or may be connected to a specific religion or belief system.

economic Relating to the production and distribution of wealth. Countries with strong economies often have wealthier citizens than those with weak economies.

empires Large areas of land or many countries that are under the rule of one person. At one time, the Romans ruled an empire that covered much of Europe.

enlightened despots Absolute monarchs who tried to improve their subjects' lives by giving them some rights; they are also referred to as enlightened absolutists.

Saudi Arabia

entrepreneur A person who takes a personal business risk in the hope of making a profit. Many entrepreneurs battle large obstacles, such as poverty or a lack of education, and still make their businesses succeed.

ethnic Relating to people who share a common culture, background, or race. Even if people come from the same country, they may have different ethnic backgrounds.

executive branch The branch of government concerned with making sure laws are carried out and obeyed.

human rights Rights believed to belong universally to every person, such as the right to live and to speak freely without fear of detention or torture from a government.

legislative Relating to the lawmaking powers of government. In many countries, a parliament is the legislature, or lawmaking body.

nobility In some societies, the name given to a class of people who are regarded as socially superior, often because of connections to wealth or royalty. When not referred to as a group, individuals are called nobles.

parliament A group of officials elected to make laws in a country. Many countries in Europe have a parliament.

republic A form of government in which government officials represent citizens. Republics are often, but not always, democratic.

BIBLIOGRAPHY

Bentley, Jerry H., and Herbert F. Ziegler. *Traditions and Encounters*. 2 Vols. Boston: McGraw-Hill, 2003.

Central Intelligence Agency. *The World Factbook 2006*. http://www.cia.gov/cia/publications/factbook

Gifford, Clive. *1,000 Years of Famous People*. New York: Kingfisher, 2002.

Krieger, Joel, ed. *The Oxford Companion to Politics of the World*. New York: Oxford University Press, 1993.

Pious, Richard M. *Governments of the World*. 3 Vols. New York: Oxford University Press, 1998.

Wingate, Philippa. *Kings and Queens*. London: Usborne Publishing, 1995.

INDEX

Published by Creative Education

P.O. Box 227, Mankato, Minnesota 56002

Creative Education is an imprint of The Creative Company.

Design by Rita Marshall

Printed in the United States of America

Photographs by Alamy Images (TIM GRAHAM, Mary Evans Picture Library,

Popperfoto, V&A Images, Visual Arts Library), Bridgeman Art Library

(Chessmen given to Samuel Pepys (1633-1703) by King James II (1633-

1701), English School, (17th century) / © Museum of London, UK, Portrait of

Marie-Antoinette de Habsbourg-Lorraine (1755-93) (oil on canvas), French

School, (18th century) / Musée Antoine Lecuyer, Saint-Quentin, France),

Corbis (Archivo Iconographico, Bettmann, Tim Brakemeier,

Christie's Images, HO), Getty Images (AFP, Hulton Archive,

Tim Graham, Imagno / Austrian Archives, Time Life Pictures)

Copyright © 2008 Creative Education

United Kingdom

Library of Congress Cataloging-in-Publication Data

Fandel, Jennifer. Monarchy / by Jennifer Fandel.

p. cm. — (Forms of government)

Includes index.

ISBN-13: 978-1-58341-534-4

1. Monarchy. I. Title.

JC375.F36 2007   321'.6—dc22   2006020153

First edition

2 4 6 8 9 7 5 3 1

GUARDS OUTSIDE BUCKINGHAM PALACE